Like a Shoe That Pinches

*How I Found Serenity Through
The 12-Step Program of Emotions Anonymous*

Like a Shoe That Pinches

*How I Found Serenity Through
The 12-Step Program of Emotions Anonymous*

Carrie Connelly

Old Mountain Press

Published by:
Old Mountain Press, Inc.
2542 S Edgewater Dr.
Fayetteville, NC 28303

www.oldmp.com

© 1999 Carrie Connelly

ISBN: 1-884778-66-6
Library of Congress Catalog Card Number: 99-63060

Like a Shoe that Pinches: How I Found Serenity Through The 12-Step Program of Emotions Anonymous.

Printed and bound in the United States of America All rights reserved Except for brief excerpts used in reviews, no portion of this work may be reproduced or published without expressed written permission from the author or the author's agent

First Edition
Manufactured in the United States of America
1 2 3 4 5 6 7 8 9 10

Prologue

Emotions Anonymous (EA) is a twelve-step program started in 1971 to offer help to those suffering from emotional problems. It is roughly based on the Alcoholics Anonymous Big Book, published in 1939, but addresses more specifically those who feel out of control of their emotional lives. Currently there are about 1,300 chapters of EA in 39 countries, and the program is administered by the EA International Services Center in St. Paul, Minnesota. Most EA groups are fairly small and host weekly meetings for members. Although the program is not religious, it is spiritual and encourages members to reflect deeply on their own relationships with "a power greater than themselves." EA includes references to the powerlessness of individuals over their emotions, but this is in fact an admission that a power greater than themselves directs the course of their lives and emotions, and the individual's job is to live in accordance with this universal will. Emotions Anonymous offers more than 50 publications for sale to those interested in the EA message or in starting their own EA group. Samples of this literature, key facets of the program, as well as contact addresses and phone numbers for those interested in finding out more, are included in the epilogue.

In accordance with EA's central concepts, no one speaks for the organization as a whole. Anonymity is important to ensure that the ego of one individual does not overwhelm the goals of the group. Therefore my story – a story of 15 years as a member of EA — is mine alone, and does not represent EA International or its chapters. Nor do I use real names, including my own, throughout the book. My story could be anyone's, however. It might well be yours or that of someone you love. It is not dramatic or sensational; it is not a story of recovery from substance abuse. But because, 15 years ago, my life became "like a shoe that pinches,"(an old EA slogan) I turned to this program and found help. I dedicate this book to those who are also searching, as I was, for that little bit of serenity that makes life livable.

Do not be overcome by evil but overcome evil with good.
-Romans 12.22

Chapter I

During a long, slow jog around my block on a pretty fall day, my life changed. And I hardly noticed at the time.
I was living in a suburb of an historic South Carolina city and working at a state agency as a public relations professional. I was young and single, restless in the way 26-year-olds are, but fairly content with my golden retriever puppy, my sometimes-boyfriends and my rental home, which I shared with my new roommate, Marian. I was far from the midwestern city where I'd been born and raised and that my family still called home, but not too far from the southern university where I'd graduated with my journalism degree at the age of 23.
I had friends, attended church, argued with my mother over the phone, never had much extra money and spent too much time at the beach, like most of the people I knew, but most of them didn't seem to have a small voice in the back of their heads telling them something was missing. For me, as the years passed, that voice was becoming louder. I was having trouble figuring out what I wanted in life, what my goals should be, where I was going, who I really was and what my relationship was to the universe. I was still recovering from what I thought of as a nervous breakdown suffered during my first job out of college a couple years earlier. It had scared the heck out of me and left me 30 pounds lighter, with a bad case of insomnia and frequent "blue moods" that I had a hard time shaking. I reminded

myself of a person with a bad hangover, but as an infrequent social drinker and a person afraid to even try narcotics, I knew that substance abuse wasn't my problem. But those AA'ers did have a certain something...

Marian had moved in just two months before and we almost instantly became friends. With her pretty, dark hair and eyes, beautiful complexion, and wonderful personality, as well as her brains and her spiritual side, we were probably destined to hit if off. Although she had a more active social life than I did (cocktail parties and dinner were required of her in her sales job) we still tried to manage some time together during the week. Sometimes that meant a jog around the block, a walk with my dog, Gertrude, or, a few times, she took me along to one of her AA meetings. She was recovering from five lost years of drinking and drugging, holding down her first steady job, and making her first set of friends that didn't "use." The local AA-ers all knew her, and she was an inspirational speaker, giving "leads" all around town at various meetings. Leads, as I learned, were tales told about what you were like before AA, what you're like now, and what happened to get you there.

I found that most of the AA members I talked to seemed genuine, intuitive and deeply spiritual. They were interested not only in who I was, what I did for a living, and where I shopped, but in discussing heart-matters that were the hallmark of only my very closest friendships. It was like they had a magnifying glass trained on my soul and saw that all was not well there – and yet I never felt violated or challenged by this, only supported in my quest. Although I had always been more of a loner than a "joiner," these people impressed me. They were positive. They were survivors.

Marian saw how much I enjoyed the company of her friends and often invited me to dinners and parties. It was here that I learned the lingo of the twelve-step programs. The steps interested me intellectually, too — as a former psychology student, I wondered how this type of introspection could lead to abstinence in the way it so surely had among these people. I met men who had lost their jobs, families and homes, woke up stoned and sleeping over a heating grate, and one morning decided it was time for a change. Women who had slept with anyone who had a good supply of booze and reefer, who had had five or six abortions, who were not only drinkers and druggers, but bulimic, anorexic or obese. I began to hear about Gamblers Anonymous, Overeaters Anonymous, Narcotics Anonymous, Co-Dependents Anonymous, Adult Children of Alcoholics. I met people who were abused as children and had become abusers themselves for a time. Now some of them had 10, 12, 20 years of recovery under their belts. These were people who, like me during the depths of my nervous breakdown, had actually feared life more than death.

And one Saturday afternoon, as Marian and I were walking off a two-mile jog around our neighborhood, she dropped a bomb.

"Carrie, seems like you've been feeling down a lot lately," she began. " I know you get something out of our AA meetings, and I just heard about a program called Emotions Anonymous. There's a group somewhere in town – maybe you could give them a call."

A key turned in my head and heart. That was all it took.

God, grant me the serenity to accept the things I cannot change, the courage to change the things I can, and the wisdom to know the difference.
- *Serenity Prayer*

Chapter II

It was easy to find EA once I knew it existed. I was volunteering one day a week as a crisis telephone counselor and that office contained all the resources I needed to track down this elusive group. The question was how could I make myself wait patiently for that Tuesday evening meeting? And what would I find once I got there? Could I blend in with the crowd or would I stand out as a newcomer? Would these people all be much older than me and would that matter? What was I getting myself into?

As I took phone calls that evening from alcoholics down on their luck, manic depressive who'd taken themselves off medication, suicidal teens popping their parents' pills, I thought about how many people in this world could benefit from a program that helps us cope with the root of so many problems — emotional disability. I rested on the crisis office couch that Saturday night and waited for dawn.

Tuesday evening found me roaming the city, lost, as usual. I glanced at my watch – late. Late for my first meeting. I located the small office building, finally, tapped on the door to the meeting room and peeked in hoping to see a crowd into which I could disappear. No such luck. Here were six older women nursing Styrofoam cups of coffee; one of the women had obviously been crying. I wanted to turn and run, but forced myself to return their greetings, find a seat, fumble with the books and literature they handed to me, smile as if I was okay.

"We were just finishing introductions, dear. Would you care to introduce yourself? I'm Anne, and I'm powerless over my emotions," said a thin, graceful matron in her 50's.

"I'm Carrie and .... well, I guess I'm powerless over my emotions, too," I managed. "This is my first meeting." Coincidentally, the group was working on step one that evening, so I opened my book and followed along through the beginning of the program. A little voice in my mind kept asking, "What is this? Will it help me? How can it help me?" and I wanted to stop time for a moment, digest all the reading material in front of me, and start again. I made myself stay tuned in to what was going on around me, knowing that, as Anne whispered to me right after I'd sat down, "There'll be time for me to answer all your questions after the meeting."

We took turns reading from a small yellow pamphlet that seemed to me to contain so much wisdom: "Just for today I choose to believe that I can live this one day," "This too shall pass," and more. Although I was familiar with the steps from my AA experiences, EA's step one hit me hard – "We admitted we were powerless over our emotions, that our lives had become unmanageable." Unmanageable. That's it, I said to myself, that's what I'm looking for – ways in which to manage my life instead of having it manage me.

The word "powerless" didn't trouble me as much as it did some people. I firmly believe in setting, planning for and achieving goals but have always had a sense of myself as a cog in the universal wheel. I consider myself an independent, free-thinking person – a feminist, even – whose always sided with the women and minorities fighting for their full piece of the pie. I've managed to live with the concept of a power greater than myself while at the same time believing in my own power to live life to its full potential.

And my emotions – well, let's just say the harder I tried to control them, the more confused I became. I could bury them, I could ignore them, I could have a pity party to honor them, but I couldn't control them. I was sick of allowing them to control me, and EA offered me a solution. I could call a truce – admit I was powerless over these waves of feeling that compelled me to be so needy that I was willing to sleep with men I barely knew, to hold resentments toward my family for a rocky upbringing, to sense only hopelessness about the future, to swallow my anger instead of learning to express it correctly. I could (I'd read ahead to step two) instead come to believe that a power greater than myself could restore me to sanity. I could allow my battered self-esteem to heal. I could acquire a feeling of security within myself, where now there was only a black hole. That, to me, would be the ultimate liberation, the most powerful feeling I could imagine. In some strange organic way, I sensed the innate power of admitting my weaknesses.

My secrets – the hate, the anger, the sadness, the resentments – were killing me, so it made sense to bare my soul, take away the power of these secrets, and allow a fresh breeze to blow through, allowing me to adopt a new way of life in which I would be more rigorously honest with myself and others. No one escapes a difficult life, no one escapes pain, no one can dodge resentments, we all have a past that we can either accept and move on or allow to consume us. In walking through the door to my first EA meeting, I was declaring war on letting these things ambush me with depression, anxiety and regret. By the end of that meeting I was still somewhat confused and hesitant, but I also sensed that heady feeling of exhilaration that comes when all your decisions are made and you now must take action.

The concessions of the weak are the concessions of fear.
-Edmund Burke

Chapter III

The room was quiet now, all the other EA members having said their "hello's" to me and left for home. I was reading a blue pamphlet about choosing a sponsor, or mentor, within EA and the advantages this offered to newcomers, while Anne was putting away meeting materials and tidying up. I instantly knew that a sponsor would be crucial to me in this program. I needed someone to push me, someone to make me face my fears and move on. Someone who knew the ropes.

"So, I'll bet you've got questions," Anne said. I did have questions, hundreds of them: Why did I always feel different than everyone else, why was I sad so often, why did I seem to lack goals and foundations, why did I allow my fears to overcome my hopes? I didn't think Anne could help me address these, though, so instead I said, "Well, I think I'm in the right place. This program can help me. It's just a matter of slowing myself down and taking it all in. I feel like I want to stay up all night reading this book and do all twelve steps by tomorrow!"

"That's not an uncommon response," Anne told me. "You find something that helps and you want it to help right away. I always say, 'God give me patience, and give it to me NOW,'" she laughed. "You just have to remember that it took you years to make yourself the person you are today, it'll take years to trade those old thoughts and behaviors for new ones. Maybe a sponsor could help."

"That would be great – I was hoping you could sponsor me, if you aren't working with too many others right now."

"Actually, my 'sponsee' just got married and moved away, so I'd be glad to sponsor you. First things first, though. Let's see ... here's your phone number," – she referred to a sign-in sheet that had members first names and telephones – "I'll write it down in my book. You need to buy an EA book and write down not only my name and number, but a couple others'. I'd like you to call me daily for a while, and make one extra call a week to the member of your choice. Telephone contact and meeting attendance are important in the program. It's fine if you decide to do lots of reading from the book and these newcomer pamphlets I'm giving you, but once you make up your mind to start on the steps, we'll have to slow down a bit. I want you to read a step, think about it, give me a call. Read the next step, think about it, give me a call. I've been in the program for six years and I've worked all the steps, so I'd like you to let me help you through it. In return, you'll help me grow in the program, because sponsoring is a way for me to deepen my understanding of the steps."

She paused and looked at me. "Hmmm ... you seem...."

"Overwhelmed," I finished. "And fearful, a little."

"Oh, fear – don't get me started on fear. That's what brings most of us through those doors to our first meeting. We'll talk a lot about your fears, both rational and irrational, and how they shape your thought processes. For now, just reassure yourself that you've made the first important step to a new way a life, a life much more free from fear than you can imagine possible," she gave me a hug. "Welcome. You're in the right place. Keep coming back."

We can learn to live with problems we cannot solve and receive the priceless gift of serenity.
-Emotions Anonymous Meeting Guide

Chapter IV

I kept trying not to cry on my drive home from the meeting, but finally I had to pull over and let it out. I was so proud of myself for not sobbing during the meeting, but those tears couldn't be held back forever. I was happy and I was relieved... I had found others like myself, with whom I was unconditionally accepted and loved. Most importantly, despite my fears, I felt hope. Hope for a life with chronic medical conditions, hope that I could come to terms with a messy past rather than reliving it in my nightmares, hope for an existence free of the compulsive thoughts and actions that made getting out of bed in the morning almost impossible.

Anne had read from the meeting guide that EA members could learn to live with unsolvable problems. I didn't understand how this was possible, how to give up the obsessive worrying about my problems that destroyed many of my days. But I trusted Anne and the other members, and they said it was so. In a leap of faith – which marks, in my experience, every successful 12-step-program member – I believed it could happen. I still had that tiny reservoir of faith in my fellow man and my God that allowed me to think that the promises offered by the program could come true for me if I but worked the program to the best of my ability. As I mopped up my tears and offered up this belief to the power of a group I thought could help me, I felt a warm wave of peaceful confidence sweep over me – a feeling I now know to be serenity.

No, my problems didn't go away or my life become easier right away, and yes, despite this peaceful feeling, the enormity of the task ahead of me – undertaking an entirely new way of life – overwhelmed me when I let it. In the coming days, between frequent telephone calls to Anne, we fought not to let it. One evening, as that first long week dragged on, I packed up my dog, my bible and my new EA book and drove down to watch the setting sun at the beach. I read, I cried, I thought, "How can I possibly find the strength to do this?" My answer came almost immediately: I couldn't proceed in my development as a compassionate human being UNLESS I did this. I had to come to understand not only my pain, but also the pain of others out there suffering from emotional turmoil. I must help myself then try to help them. It was like going to the dentist – I could dread the pain and obsess about the drill all I wanted, but in the end I had to swallow my pride and take the actions needed to get well. Might as well skip the dread and obsession and jump right into the actions if the end results were going to be the same.

Darkness fell as I bundled my wet dog and slightly soggy books into the car for the trip home.

It is only with the heart that one can see rightly; what is essential is invisible to the eye.
-Antoine de Saint-Exupery

Chapter V

The buzz I'd gotten from my first EA meeting was wearing off by the time the next Tuesday rolled around. I had, as promised, stayed up all night and read through the literature. I'd made the phone calls. I'd completed – with Anne's help – step one. But I felt a need for the fellowship of other members and a hunger to hear their stories. I wanted to know how they went about "letting go and letting God," how they take "one day at a time," whether any of the promises of the program (see Epilogue) had come true for them. Mostly, though, I was hoping to recapture that fleeting feeling of serenity I experienced after my first meeting. I needed another "hit" of that particular drug to help me face step two, which involved coming to believe that a power greater than myself could restore me to sanity.

My real trouble was with the word sanity. I had never considered myself insane – maybe a little off-kilter, maybe a little depressed and anxious, but not insane. I was to learn that EA's version of sanity is sane thinking, common sense, reasonable behavior. Insanity is not craziness, but is the process of repeating the same actions or behaviors over and over while expecting different results each time, or of indulging in "acting out" that includes temper tantrums, uncontrolled anger, compulsiveness, and lack of moderation in daily living. Following this definition, I came to terms with that pesky word and prepared to listen with open ears and an open heart to my fellow members.

I located the meeting room without incident and was less concerned about walking in and saying hello. Also, my fears over what I might or might not have in common with the six older women sitting around the table were evaporating. I was learning, through Anne, that age, sex, religious preference and background make little difference if the problems you are suffering from are pervasive and universal. Our concern for our emotional stability was enough common ground for us to stand on. During the discussion phase of this meeting on step two, I learned that these people – like the AA'ers I knew – were also survivors. Some had recently been released from mental hospitals, were experiencing severe depression that medication couldn't touch or had just lost a child or spouse. Others were simply suffering from the nagging assaults of daily life – the car that broke down, the boss who was a tyrant, the medical bills that were piling up. For most of them, getting up in the morning, making that first cup of coffee and organizing their thoughts to begin another day was the sanity they were seeking. They were placing their faith in a power greater than themselves to stop them from flying off the handle at their daughter-in-law, from spending the day in bed, from making the bad decisions that characterized their life before EA. I found I had quite a bit to add to the discussion when it was my turn to share my reflections on step two, and was pleased as heads nodded in agreement with my ideas. I felt like I belonged.

Later that evening, on the phone with Anne, I admitted that I was ready to take step two and move on to the third step – making a decision to turn my will and my life over to the care of God as I understood Him.

Decision-making, in general, had become very difficult for me. I seemed to have a blurry, romanticized perception of reality and of my own human limitations and this combination was dangerous. For example, a couple years earlier I had found myself with a boyfriend pointing a gun at my head, threatening to kill himself and me because "that's what the voices were telling him to do." My response was to take the gun, throw it away and check him into a hospital – all rational decisions – but then I redoubled my efforts to prove that I was the girl who could turn his life around. I thought I could change others (and change situations) simply by my force of will.

Meanwhile, I was falling apart emotionally. I could barely turn my car around, no less turn my – or anyone else's – life around. God seemed to be on my side, though, bailing me out before my poor decisions became poor life-choices. I always landed the job before my last $10 ran out, left the troubled boy before the boy became my husband. I needed God in my corner for sure, now, as I made a decision to turn my will and my life over.

I felt certain that God could take better care of my life than I had, but it troubled me to always think of God as a Him. My God wasn't necessarily a Him but a Her or an It or a Them, everywhere and anywhere, any-sex or no-sex. Even my old standby the Catholic Church had modified its sexist language – why couldn't EA? I turned to the EA book for what would have to suffice as an answer: "In EA literature, we use gender-neutral language. However, in the steps and traditions God is referred to in masculine terms because AA views these as historic writings that should remain unchanged." And, of course, EA literature is all derived from AA.

As Anne pointed out in conversations later in the week, making a decision to do something is not the same as actually doing it. It was only through prayer, meditation, meetings and member contacts that I could keep my nose out of my own business and turn my life over to God. I promised to follow through, completed my third step and became ready "for the vigorous actions of step four."

Be not afraid of life. Believe that life is worth living, and your belief will help create the fact.
-*William James*

Chapter VI

I took a breather to review my progress so far in EA – three steps in three weeks, and already I felt a "new freedom and happiness," as stated in the twelve promises. I was making the baby steps toward change. I was now supplementing my EA get-togethers with a weekly AA meeting, since I needed that extra boost mid-week and my EA fellowship had few local chapters. I found more than ever in common with my AA friends, but the contrast between the programs led me to count my blessings – I didn't have the burdens, the cravings that substance abuse caused. And yet ... staying away from booze was at least a tangible thing, measurable day by day. Turning my life over to God was more subtle and slippery. I could and often did "fall off the wagon" by taking my worries back out of God's hands and again into my own. I liked that feeling of obsessive worry, in some ways. It was comforting and familiar, like your favorite pair of shoes with a hole worn through the bottom. If I were to give this up, what would take its place?

Steps four through ten were there to answer that question. But these were the tough steps, the meat of the EA program, the ones that would have to be taken gradually and even then, sometimes only partially completed. They involved taking measure of my entire life, making lists, naming names, tackling embarrassing apologies, submerging myself in the grease pits where I'd tossed inappropriate sexual conduct, youthful lusts and longings, greed, envy, pride and hatred. The eighth grade, when I told my best friend that she couldn't be seen with me anymore because it was affecting my popularity? That was there. Cutting myself off from my family for my own selfish reasons when they needed me? Ditto. Taking digs at my own self-esteem, which had eroded my confidence over the years? You bet. And, I learned, making amends to yourself was sometimes the toughest job in the program.

Gradually, as time passed in EA, I began to recognize that the things I least wanted to do, the steps that seemed the most onerous, were exactly the correct steps to take. This was the beginning of "trusting my gut," another familiar EA phrase, and it is from this trust that I developed a feeling of security within myself. God was slipping me a cheat sheet on life's toughest tests, as long as I took the time to look for it.

The small voice that had once questioned the meaning of my past and the value of my future was growing up, and in time I would learn to trust its judgement, rather than the pronouncement of the dozens of psychology and self-help books under my bed that diagnosed me with this or that syndrome and directed the cure. For me, these books and their self-assured authors and gurus had opened my eyes to some new ideas but had never helped me get "unstuck." They relied on willpower and personal determination, which believe me, I had plenty of, and yet these qualities were not what started me down the path to serenity. EA had what I needed and I needed to only trust that it could help.

We are punished by our sins, not for them.
-Elbert Hubbard

Chapter VII

Over time I began to think that step four, making a searching and fearless moral inventory, was not as daunting to me as it seemed to be for others I'd talked to. I was becoming an expert at mentally cataloguing my shortcomings, so, as I expected, writing it all down was not difficult. The problem was that Anne had said I should list one positive for every negative in my inventory, and this indeed slowed me down. What was positive about me? I came up with a couple items suggested to me by friends – my sense of humor, my smarts, my love of animals, my compassion for others – and it became somewhat easier. These lists were lengthy, scratched-out and written over many times, a jumble of paper fragments bundled into my daily journal. And I can't say that the 'step five' thought of sharing anything so personal – even with Anne – made me happy. God knew me, I knew myself, but Anne ... she just knew that I was a shy newcomer struggling with my emotions. I thought she might be shocked by some of my inventory, that it would change her opinion of me. Step five was the first test of the new sense of trust in others that I'd been developing since my initial meeting.

As I sat sharing my inventory with her at her kitchen table late one evening, I relieved to see that her expression didn't change as I read – she didn't frown or sigh or shake her head or act judgmental in any way. She just listened in a simple and caring way I'd never experienced before. And when I finished she thanked me for allowing her to share the intimate details of my life and reassured me that, as a veteran EA members, she'd "heard it all before." She empathized with the sad parts of my story, praised me for doing a thorough fourth and fifth step and making such fine progress in the program, and hugged me goodbye.

Some EA members say they are overcome by a sense of peace after doing their fourth and fifth steps. I felt a certain quiet in my soul, coupled with an odd combination of exhaustion and energy. I was exhausted with the pace at which my life was "morphing" but energized by the changes taking place in me. I was experiencing an emotional thaw after years and years of having frozen my feelings, and I found I was needing more rest, more sleep, more quiet time to take it all in. These steps had exposed the defects in my character that had allowed me to make my life difficult, to cloud my decision-making ability, to overcome my moral reasoning with impulsive actions. In time I was ready to move on to step six, becoming entirely ready to have God remove all my defects of character.

First, though, I had to admit that all my foibles, some of which I'd relied on to survive, were really defects. I didn't like this word. Some of my character traits were obviously flaws – my impetuousness, impatience, neediness – but they made me ME. I was vulnerable, playful, willing to come to anyone's rescue, empathetic. It seemed that these traits were all intertwined and I wasn't sure who I would be if I turned them all over to God.

Anne came to my rescue. She pointed out that the sixth step does not say we have to give up being who we are. It says we have to become ready for God to push the delete button on the characteristics that He/She thinks are getting in our way. But, like primping for a prom or a party, getting ready to do something can often take more time than actually doing it. I would have to marshal all my patience and listen to God for clues on when I was ready. I put an ear to the ground and prepared to listen carefully.

Healing is a matter of time, but it is sometimes also a matter of opportunity.
-Hippocrates

Chapter VIII

It's funny how the simple process of focusing your attention on an issue can change you. I'd always been an introspective person and felt I'd lived an "examined life," but now I was seeing that huge portions of my life were lived on autopilot. If I really thought that all of us were God's children, for example, would I have gossiped about a friend's unwed pregnancy? If I sensed that others were struggling to interpret life as I was, would I scheme to overthrow my boss as office manager? And how about my family? My mom was constantly sending me clippings from the Help Wanted ads up north, which I trashed without reading. Maybe I shouldn't be so hasty. Maybe the people I love do have my best interests at heart and deserve at least considerate attention. They are people, too, struggling to get through each day just as I was. Maybe we all have more in common than I'd thought. This was the start of sifting through my personality traits, looking for assets and defects, in a way I'd never before considered. This was God telling me, "It's time."

And as I became ready to have God remove my defects of character, I felt an immense sadness for the time I'd wasted and the people I'd unknowingly hurt. This remorse was not for big crimes – no murder or mayhem on my list – and yet it was pervasive.

I thought that if I'd only been able to know myself better, to be scrupulously honest with myself and others, my life would have been better lived.

When I shared these thoughts with Anne, she commiserated. "You think you feel sad? Imagine me coming into the program with more than half my life lived. You've got to turn it around and be grateful that, despite all the water under the bridge, you can start again now," she said.

This grieving process, I found, was cleansing. We aren't allowed to go back and relive our lives, after all, so perhaps dealing honestly with our regrets, resolving to do better, and moving on was the next best thing. In the face of these emotions, I discovered that an entirely new aspect of myself was emerging – humility. Oh, sure, I had been humble in the way the world thinks of it. I had been a doormat, I had allowed my self-esteem to erode, I had felt inferior to others, but true humility is not that. It is, according to the EA book, having a clear view of reality and seeing the truth about ourselves.

I began to feel more confident about taking steps six and seven, becoming ready to have God remove all of our defects of character and humbly asking Him to remove our shortcomings. It didn't happen overnight and it wasn't accompanied by a clap of thunder and a voice from above, but a new me was slowly taking shape. I was both proud of the transformation and humbled by the process, but most of all, I was thankful that this pain had a purpose and signaled the start of healing.

By this time, several months had passed since I'd started attending EA. I was becoming more confident and knowledgeable in the program and felt good about sharing with newcomers – few and far between for our little group, but important nonetheless – what I'd learned. On my three-month anniversary, Anne and the other members baked me a cake and had a little party after the meeting. As I blew out the candles, Anne whispered in my ear, "Remember – progress, not perfection. You're doing great!"

If I have seen further it is by standing on the shoulders of giants.
-*Isaac Newton*

Chapter IX

Anything worth doing is worth doing right – was my family motto. And by right I mean perfectly, or over and over again until as close to perfection as possible. My father would check to make sure the stove was shut off two or three times before leaving the house and one of us would always have to jump out of the car before family trips to make absolutely sure the front door was locked. I became an obsessive-compulsive adult, overly focused on cleanliness and order. And although as I grew into my twenties I dreamed of marriage and family, I wondered if I was too set in my ways to compromise. I knew that having another person in my life would mean not always getting my way, and that children prevent a house from being perfectly clean. So much would be out of my control, how could I handle it?

I didn't know. But God did. And so began my efforts to replace perfection with "good enough," persistence with "take a break and have some fun," self-determination with "ask someone for help." These attitudes applied to my EA program, too. No one can live a perfect life, and to try to do so would be at the expense of those you care for and your own serenity. I wasn't perfect and God still loved me. Maybe I could loosen up and learn to love myself again.

I also longed for a certain consistency in my life. I wanted to be a consistently caring, empathetic, thoughtful person without the huge mood swings that marred so many of my days, so I began to practice an old EA tradition that says, "Fake it before you make it." I would get out of bed each morning, say the Serenity Prayer and ask God to use my will to his service, dress as carefully as I could, be as pleasant as possible with everyone I met, slow down when I felt like rushing and smile when I felt like crying. It took a huge amount of energy to act as if I was already the person I wanted to be, and I didn't always succeed. But I did slowly retrain myself to focus outward rather than inward; to really listen to what others were saying and put myself in their place; to stop dwelling on my own life, my own problems. As a veteran AA member, my roommate Marian often set me back on track when I was ruminating on a particular issue.

"You're not turning that over, Carr. I can tell by that worried look on your face. If you can't do it, God can, so let Him," she'd say. What a blessing it was to be surrounded by so many caring 12-step members in my life! I'm sure this contributed to my early enthusiasm and continued commitment to a program that will be my partner for life.

It also inspired me to strive for maturity in the program, something that only comes with time and repeated practice of the steps, because I saw how members with many years as 12-steppers seemed to live charmed lives. Not that they were always lucky or successful – in fact it was sometimes the opposite, they would become quite poor in material goods yet rich in spirit. But they seemed to have a God-given intuition that led them to make the choices that were right for them, God was doing for them what they had not been able to do alone. I could always tell a person who had a small, secret pocket of serenity to retreat to when the world was hard to bear. I wanted to be that kind of person.

A man should never be ashamed to own he has been in the wrong, which is but saying, in other words, that he is wiser today than he was yesterday.
-Alexander Pope

Chapter X

I approached step eight warily: Make a list of all persons I had harmed, and become willing to make amends to them all. Had I really harmed many people, beside myself? I hate apologizing, particularly years after the fact. The thought made my stomach turn. Also, this was a difficult step for many reasons — it wasn't as easy as going through my moral inventory and making a list. I had to think about the concept of "harm," had to consider who was accessible and who wasn't, had to decide if there was an acceptable way to make amends to those I would finally place on my list.

That list did turn out to be fairly short, but also very complicated. There were people of all walks of life, all ages and economic backgrounds, relatives and non-relatives, people scattered throughout the country. I'd long lost touch with some of these folks and was baffled by the prospect of making amends to them. A careful reading of the step stopped my fears from ballooning too much – I had, indeed, made a list. Now I had to work on willingness. That's all this step calls for. This is one time I was not tempted to look ahead to the next step — the next step was into a deep pit, or so I feared. I had to stop here for a while and pray for the willingness to open my eyes and move ahead.

When we did steps eight and nine (making amends) in meetings I'd been amazed at member's tales of asking for forgiveness for unforgivable acts and receiving it. Or, likewise, apologizing to the back of someone's head that wouldn't even turn around to look at you, no less forgive you. And there were many, many stories about the complex nature of forgiveness — how one must change one's ways for good and prove by actions that the apology is sincere. After all, you can't wipe out ten years of drinking, drugging or abusing with a simple, "Sorry about that." And what about compulsive gamblers who stole to support their habit? Money was part of the restitution they needed to make. If you'd wasted a portion of someone's life by your poor judgement, maybe you needed to pay them back by being there for them both physically and emotionally, above and beyond the call of duty, for a while to come. This was heavy stuff. The entire EA program was a commitment to a new way of life, of course, but did it have to be this difficult? The thought of making amends seemed to me more of an admission of defeat than a renewal of hope.

And, of course, the top name on my amends list was my own. How was I to go about making amends to myself? Anne said this involved being gentler and more forgiving with myself, taking time to indulge myself once in a while, freeing myself from feelings of guilt by dwelling on positives rather than negatives, practicing — and learning to enjoy — moderation and balance in my life. She might as well have told me to go out and build a house by myself, for all the skills I had in these things.

For the first time since I'd started in the program, I felt unequal to the task of moving beyond the step I'd just taken. This is called "plateauing,' and it's fairly common among those of us who dive into EA headfirst and expect to meet with nothing but success in working one step after another. It felt like a giant stop sign. I was scared.

No passion so effectually robs the mind of all its powers of acting and reasoning as fear.
-*Edmund Burke*

Chapter XI

I hate that big, black hole that threatens to swallow me up during my weakest moments. And it takes so little to trigger my fear response – someone not answering back when I call out hello, the unreturned phone call, the offhand remark that I misinterpret, a broken date, missing out on that raise at work. For the first 20 years of my life, fear was my biggest single motivator. I was tough on the outside and fearful on the inside. I had fears about financial ruin; I feared cancer and other debilitating diseases; I feared being too close to someone as well as not being close enough to anyone; I feared failure; I feared loneliness; I feared I wasn't good enough for the men I was dating; I was afraid of the dark; I was terrified of death.

Once I gave in to one fear, the others would flock around me like vultures around a dying animal. I had repetitive nightmares of being broke and alone, living on the streets, elderly and sad. My fears paralyzed me. And yet, I was a bright, sophisticated, generally successful person with a loving and supportive family and friends. Only rarely had I been denied things I truly wanted and worked for. I didn't have a track record of failure and ruin – why did I fear it so? This was the start of facing and resolving my many, many unreasonable fears, perhaps the greatest gift the EA program would ever give me. I longed to be able to say, with confidence, the EA "Just for Today" saying that goes, "Just for today I shall be unafraid. Particularly, I shall be unafraid to enjoy what is good, what is beautiful, and what is lovely in life."

And there is so very much that is lovely in life! I felt as if life was passing me by – I couldn't enjoy its wonder because fear held me in its grip. I wanted to be able to attend a concert and soar with the lyric notes of a classical piece. I wanted to pay attention to where I was, what I was doing, what people were saying to me, and turn off the whirring sounds of fear that reverberated in my mind day and night. I didn't want to become a perennially anxious person who prefers caution to love and safety to satisfaction.

I felt that God was calling me to conquer my fears and dare to take on life on its own terms, to be bold and self-confident, to dare to have dreams and then to work to make them come true. In other words, to learn to love myself. And then to learn to love others – and life – just as I loved myself. I had precedent for success in my life and there was no reason I couldn't extend that success to tackling my fears. The program emboldened me to take those first, small steps toward freedom from fear. What I wanted at my center, after all, was not a big, black pit but the bright light of serenity. There is hope.

I started by making detailed lists of my fears and the responses they elicited in me. That long, long list, in itself, was laughable and gave me a bit of distance from these fears. I would have to train myself to recognize when I was falling into the fear trap and devise a method – a call to my sponsor? The serenity prayer? A meeting? – to stop myself. Without this new courage I was working toward, I knew I would not be able to progress in the program.

I also knew it would be the hardest-won, and best, gift I could give myself.

In a real dark night of the soul it is always three o'clock in the morning.
– F. Scott Fitzgerald

Chapter XII

My sponsor, Anne, helped me to face and rethink the painful times of my pre-EA past. What I had thought to be a nervous breakdown was, I had learned, some type of clinical depression suffered in my early twenties. The signs had been unmistakable, had I known what to look for: inability to sleep or eat, poor concentration, loss of memory, suicidal thoughts, lethargy, crying. It felt to me like one long, long day in a world without color or companionship – terrifying. I simply thought I'd broken something invisible inside me, much like I'd broken my collarbone when I was a toddler, and I needed help to fix it.

I began to look for a therapist, but was startled by their high fees and impersonal airs. At the time I was practically penniless, house-sitting for friends, working part-time at a liquor store (the most I could manage in my low-functioning state) and living on crackers and cheese supplemented with the occasional candy bar.

Finally, I knocked on the right door. Doctor Martin was a simple psychologist working from her home in the small town I lived in. Her white-and-green clapboard house was comforting to me from the outside, and inside there were overstuffed chairs, thick carpeting, too many books, and several boxes of Kleenex scattered here and there. She was gentle, soft-featured and slightly overweight. She had a beautiful voice. I sensed that she was someone who would cry with me, just as my mother had when I was stood up for a date in high school. I was right.

I had to clear up the question of payment on my first visit. It was embarrassing to grovel, but I so needed help. I had lost so much weight, my clothes hung on me, and I had dark circles under my eyes because sleep was difficult and frightening. I thought that perhaps I was dying. Dr. Martin listened carefully and proposed a solution.

"I'll see you for half-fee, Carrie, in exchange for you doing some baking for me. You told me you still enjoy experimenting with homemade breads and I've got a passion for them. Two loaves a week and we'll call it even," she said.

I was amazed and grateful. Thus I began twice-weekly sessions that, in the end, saved my life. I resisted medication – which would have helped me so much, I now realize – because when I was growing up relying on pills was seen as a sign of weakness. I wasn't weak, I was strong. I just happened to be temporarily drowning.

I'm not sure that too much in my life would have been different had I been in EA at this time. The program would likely have been too challenging for me to tackle since even getting out of bed was so hard. I could have certainly used the companionship of others who had 'been there,' though, and it would have helped me to try and get out of my own head. But serious illnesses – both physical and mental – are the domain of doctors and hospitals, I feel, and though the program can begin to change thoughts, feelings and attitudes, one can't think one's way out of depression.

Today I am a firm believer in the helpfulness of professionals and their medication. And professionals who have a working knowledge of twelve-step programs are even more valuable, since these programs can often work together with medicines and therapy to pull an individual's life back together.

As Winston Churchill (a sufferer himself) once said, depression is the black dog. It had bitten me, and I would recover, but the scars remain. EA is a balm to soothe those scars.

The years teach much which the days never know.
- Ralph Waldo Emerson

Chapter XIII

I was struggling to come to terms with my past and at the same time to live in the present. My family was coming to visit me for Thanksgiving, turnabout from our usual routine, and in between getting ready with turkey, stuffing, housecleaning and whatnot, I was nagged by a feeling of having forgotten something. During an EA meeting, it occurred to me: This would be an ideal opportunity to prepare my amends to my parents and sister. My brother, to whom I felt I owed no amends, was staying at his college through the break.

I would have the time to make amends to each of these people alone, on my own turf. I would have my sponsor and my friends here to turn to if things did not go well. And, having lived through my first amends, I would be able to progress more confidently through step nine – making direct amends to people wherever possible, except when to do so would injure them or others. I was nervous about the whole idea, but I knew I must take this action to continue my healing process.

Apologizing – particularly for years and years of behavior patterns – was hard for me to think about and nearly impossible to do well. I fumbled through a talk with my mother that began, "Mom, I know how hurt you were when I decided to go far away to school, and I just wanted to apologize for some of the hurtful things I did to you during that time..." I was met with a baffled look until I backed up a little.

"You know those meetings I go to every week? The ones I told you about that work on my emotions? Well, one of the things we have to do is make apologies for past regrets. I wanted to do that with you now. You don't have to say anything, or even forgive me, just listen. Then you can ask questions, if you want."

I hadn't told my folks all that much about EA, and my sister had heard almost nothing about it, so they were confused, to say the least. When they looked in my eyes, though, and saw how dead serious I was about this, they sat back, listened and tried to understand. I was so grateful to them, because instead of telling me I was crazy, instead of saying, "never mind, let's just go out for dessert and forget about this," they listened. In fact, I think this was the beginning of some true dialogue in our family, the opening of a box of secrets that no longer needed to be nailed shut. This gave us a framework for dealing as a family with some very turbulent and emotional times to come.

I'm not sure where I got the words to make those amends, but the words came and I felt like I was doing what I needed to do.

Both of my parents did forgive me for my list of transgressions. My sister did not, wanted proof of how I'd changed. I tried to accept both the forgiveness — and the lack of it — equally gracefully, since it was my job only to 'clean my side of the fence,' not to judge others' decisions. Thus began my lifelong commitment of making amends to my family by becoming a better me. My effort persists to this day and they are among the many reasons that I feel I'll be an EA member for the rest of my time on this planet. I must remember that I'm on a course of learning to understand myself and others to the best of my ability, to reach out in empathy, to be sensitive to pain, to be strong when I'm leaned on, to admit my weaknesses when I need help, and, most of all, to be honest and forthright in every area of my life.

How appropriate that I was able to begin my ninth step on a day known for giving thanks. I had so much to be thankful for – my life, my health, my possessions, my job, my family, my program, my faith. As I shared with each family member not only what I regretted but also what I was thankful for in their lives, it occurred to me that this step is really more about thanksgiving than forgiveness.

Admitting and apologizing for past mistakes clears out the scraggly trees of regret and allows me to see the forest of good fortune that I enjoy. I was able to fall asleep Thanksgiving night with a pleasant feeling of fullness that was not only from too much turkey and gravy, but from an abundance of blessings.

To this day, 15 years later, I am still in the process of slowly working my way through that list of amends. Life is a journey, not a destination.

Whatever your heart clings to and confides in, that is really your God.
-*Martin Luther*

Chapter XIV

I thought that perhaps the fourth step was the last time I'd have to face my character defects for a while, but I was wrong. The tenth step tells me to continue to take a personal inventory and when I'm wrong to promptly admit it. And it's logical that such a step exists, since life is messy and we all make mistakes as we go along. This step seemed easy compared to the rigors of the previous steps. I had started keeping a nightly journal as soon as I began working with my sponsor, and it was here that I listed my failings for the day – and my successes, too. If I needed to apologize for a dishonest action or catty comment, I tried to do so before the sun set; if not, I'd try to make amends the following day. This pattern continues to be important for me in my program, even though today I sometimes summarize my wrongs in prayer rather than in writing.

The tenth step feels as if God is prying open the last remaining dark corners of my life – those little nasties I try to hide from the light of each day – to allow continued healing to take place. If I forget to do it too many times, I begin to harbor self-doubt and resentment again, I start to feel as if all is not well. And believe me, as a person struggling with emotional problems, I can allow myself to feel pretty darn uncomfortable before I say my "I'm sorry's." I'm continuously arm-wrestling with God for control of my life. The only difference is that I let Him win a little more often now.

My faith has become an entirely different thing from what is was when I attended my first EA meeting. God used to be a stuffed animal I'd pull out when I needed comfort. Now my beliefs are deep, complex and pervading. They surround me all the time, like a gentle cloud, and I know I only need to fall backwards to be caught and supported and helped along. In some ways, I've become less strictly religious and increasingly spiritual. And yes, I do now have that core of serenity and strength that is as unshakeable as my faith (although I always pray that God not decide to test me too much on this!). But I don't stay strong by putting myself on autopilot — I have to continue to work on my character defects, my humility, my amends, my turning things over to God, my EA program.

I'm a voracious reader and have become even more so since EA. I feel as if I want to open my mind to all the types of people, places and experiences there are and to become as fully involved in life as I was distant from it before the program. I also still enjoy volunteer and outreach work because that is my faith made manifest.

As I began to practice step ten (a continuing personal inventory), I found my life beginning to change not only on the inside, but also on the outside. I got a new and better job, coincidentally closer to my family, which meant sad good-byes to all my EA friends, my roommate, my sponsor. And during this time of hectic preparation, I welcomed starting the eleventh step: seeking through prayer and meditation to improve my conscious contact with God as I understand him, praying only for knowledge of His will for me and the power to carry that out.

One single grateful thought raised to heaven is the most perfect prayer.
-G. E. Lessing

Chapter XV

I've always prayed – in fact, at times I've been a prayer-aholic: "God, let me have this, let me do that, save me from whatever's threatening me. Make me comfortable. Protect those I love. Provide world peace. Stop the destruction of the rainforest." On and on I would go, as if once I completed a thorough list, squeezed my eyes shut and offered it heavenward, the miracles I sought would take place.

I'm sure God is grateful for any sort of dialogue, but I now feel that these kinds of prayers characterize a somewhat childish faith. I said these prayers before I found EA, back when I thought I alone was in control of my destiny. This was a one-way conversation, and what God asks of me today involves opening my ears and shutting my mouth. The EA program taught me one complete and beautiful prayer to which I aspire: "God, I offer myself to you, to build and to do with me as you will. Help me let go of my self-centeredness, so I can better recognize your will for me. Help me overcome my difficulties so others can see how your love, wisdom and strength allows me to change. Thank you for being with me. May I do your will always."

When I am able to truly quiet my rushing thoughts and say this prayer well, I feel as if I'm lowering myself into a steamy whirlpool on a chilly day. The water laps over me, taking away my aches and pains, enveloping me in quiet warmth. I'm able to touch that core of serenity I've worked so hard to build and realize that the purpose of my life is not so much to figure out what I need from God but what God needs from me.

Most of the time what God needs me to do is perform all those boring, repetitive, everyday tasks that are the basis of work and family life in a thoughtful and loving way, but sometimes I have more challenging jobs: Confronting a friend about her alcoholism, visiting a relative in a mental hospital, scrimping to lend some money to a needy coworker. I find when I am able to live that prayer, I am better able to be a positive person, to be grateful for all that I have and to feel satisfied at day's end that I have contributed to the world around me.

I admire people who practice meditation, but as yet this is just a goal for me. I can barely sit still to pray no less to spend time meditating. And yet, the few times I did get books on the subject and began practicing, I found meditation was very helpful in quieting me. I could almost feel my blood pressure lowering, my breathing deepening. Everyday life encourages us to rush around, accumulate more and more possessions, try to do two or more things at the same time (on the cell phone while your driving, preferably), and meditation is an antidote to all that. Like prayer, it's a form of conscious contact between you and the powers of the universe. There is so much we could learn if we could only stop and listen.

As I began a new life and a new job in the Midwest, I had to force myself to stop and listen once in a while. But the EA program had given me increased confidence in turning my life over to God and I found I often intuitively knew which choices were best for me. I settled in for a short stay in my former childhood home until I could find my own place, then set about locating a nearby EA group. I was lucky enough to find a small number of veteran EA members headed by a very wise old owl – who was soon to become my new sponsor.

It is life near the bone where it is sweetest.
-Henry David Thoreau

Chapter XVI

Returning home dredged up all those childhood feelings – helplessness, powerlessness, conflicts between parents and siblings, joy and sadness – that had been long buried. My emotions had ruled me during my years at home. As a child and adolescent, I knew no better than to give them the power to do so.

Thanks to EA, I was learning that although feelings are neither good nor bad, acting on them can be. I can feel angry enough to punch someone but actually doing it is wrong. I have to find appropriate ways of recognizing and acting on my feelings – for example, I'd address anger with exercise. When I was really angry about something, I'd take a break and go for a run, pretending that each pounding step I took was leaving some of my anger embedded in the pavement. Or I'd get up a game of tennis and take it out on the ball.

The fact that I was actually feeling my emotions rather than ignoring or stuffing them was such a positive step for me. I spent years in a numb, emotionless state, afraid to really feel sadness or happiness for fear that it would overwhelm me. Anger and resentment were my enemies and rather than acknowledge them I would turn them into dark, depressed moods marked by anxiety and restlessness. Now I was learning to say to my mother, "When you play martyr like that it makes me feel so angry"; or, to a boyfriend, "I'm feeling confused about our relationship right now and I'd like to take a break." I was learning to be a little more gentle with myself, spending an afternoon resting on the couch after a particularly tough day at work, and I understood the importance of having a good, strong support group of friends and EA members around to talk to when I got stuck.

I did get stuck often during that first year back up north. I sought out professional help once again, and my weekly counseling sessions were both difficult and valuable. I was able to go back and discuss my emotional past – all those little family incidents and high-school first loves that haunted my dreams – and fend off the blue moods that threatened to conquer me. I also had to develop an adult relationship with my parents that allowed me to express myself and be helpful yet not be overwhelmed or act as a doormat for them, or to fall into those childhood patterns of rebellion and resentment. Little by little I was working to make another of the EA promises come true in my life – to not regret the past nor wish to shut the door on it.

I rediscovered friends from my youth, began dating and was learning a great deal about the craft of writing and editing from a helpful mentor and boss at work. I joined a church and reestablished relationships with my brother, sister, grandparents, aunts and uncles. I tried to 'walk the talk' of EA in all of these revived relationships and be mindful of showing the kind of respect and courtesy that I expected in return. I wasn't a teenager any more.

As I took my place with my family once again, I reawakened a longing for a family of my own. I started to think about the idea of settling down and having children with someone I loved. I knew that I had only to turn these feelings over to God and allow myself to be involved in the sorts of social activities that would lead to such a relationship, and that things would work out as they were meant to. I was learning to live life on a deeper level and that felt good. I was ready to move on to the final step in the EA program.

Those who stand for nothing fall for anything.
-Alex Hamilton

Chapter XVII

I was still a relative novice in EA, and the people in this new group were as yet strangers to me, and yet I felt very comfortable in these meetings. The group was larger and more diverse than my EA gathering down south, and I was struck again by the commonality of our emotional problems and our desire to become well. This destroyed any barriers to communication, and I found these new members were eager to learn of my experiences in a group elsewhere in the country. Shy at first, I soon began attending the "group consciousness" meetings that set the direction and tone for larger EA groups and establish rules for participation according to the twelve traditions (see Epilogue). I took a sponsor who had a decade more in the program than I and was instrumental in starting this local EA chapter. Sarah was to guide me along the last leg of my journey — realizing a spiritual awakening as a result of the steps and trying to carry the EA message and practice the principles in all my affairs.

A spiritual awakening is a gift, like faith, that can't be rushed. With Sarah's help I would have to develop maturity in my program and learn to reach out to new members, to take a more active role in the future of the group, perhaps learn to tell my own story to others who might benefit.

And, most importantly, I would have to learn to live the EA program in every area of my life, with as much consistency as I could muster. I would develop and stand on my principles, complete the formation of my character and moral values that had been evolving throughout my life, and make a plan for my future – understanding that I would create the plan and strive to achieve it yet allow God to be responsible for the results.

This was a tall order, but since I was starting my life over in a new location and with a new job, it was somewhat easier to reframe myself. I was to go from being a pessimist to an optimist, a negative person to a positive, someone who was always eager to talk to one who primarily listened; someone who tried to recognize and express feelings in an appropriate way, while at the same time turning over any overwhelming emotions to God. I wanted to be a grateful soul, living 'one day at a time,' with the understanding that life is a gift to be cherished, not a right to be taken for granted. I wanted to be an example of the kinds of changes EA can make in a person's life, so that my life would be a testament to the power of God's will.

I was realizing, too, an increasing desire to find my life's partner, to marry and have children. I was hoping that all the 'work' I'd done on myself would allow me to cultivate the kind of honest, loving, long-term relationship I aspired to. I was fortunate enough to soon realize this dream.

Let us do something beautiful for God.
- *Mother Teresa*

Chapter XVIII

If anything tested my newfound emotional strength, it was relationships. Friendships were complicated enough, family matters were a tangle of feelings, but falling in love was so much more overwhelming. I had had dozens of relationships in the past, of course, some in which I was incredibly needy, some which were emotionally abusive. Other relationships were purely physical and some were simply young love.

But what I had with Dan was something different. There was serenity in this relationship that I'd never experienced before. This man accepted me for what I was — a recovering "emotionaholic" prone to anxiety and depression — and was able to help me in the ways I needed help and celebrate the things that made me different and special. I was able, in return, to be completely open and honest in a way I never had before with other men.

It helped that we were attracted to each other, shared a Catholic upbringing, a love of books, a longing for a family, and our core values were very similar. And rather than feeling like I was tumbling into yet another foamy mass of emotions, I felt like a door was opening for me. In fact, I had dreams that included turning a knob and looking in, seeing children and a home, the things I'd wanted but thought I'd never have. My life had been a contradiction of both craving companionship and not being able to handle too much closeness. Socializing was difficult and tiring for me, crowds scared me, I never knew how to become part of the conversation in a group, parties were paralyzing. People who seemed emotionally 'normal' baffled me – how did they get up each day, prioritize their tasks, make complicated decisions, seem to fit into any situation – without all the angst I suffered? When they got mad, they said, "I'm mad." When they were sad, they cried. Then they got over it and were happy again. This was like a code I couldn't crack. Thankfully, EA was my secret decoder ring, my way in to society and mature relationships. I was lucky.

As my love for Dan grew and we began planning for the future, I realized that God was doing for me what I hadn't been able to do for myself. I was tolerating the chaos of closeness without having to be in control all the time, sharing things with a person (other than my sponsor) who was loving and non-judgmental, learning to trust on a whole new level, deepening my skills as a human being and broadening my love of life.

In the process, I became more and more able to reach out to others and learn to put my twelfth step into action. I was more open about my spirituality and felt more comfortable discussing the program with acquaintances that I thought it might help. I started to be more active in my church, attending Bible study meetings and lectures that were to help me understand the core of my formal faith.

Someone once told me that when we are happy, God is smiling; when we're sad, God cries. God was definitely smiling now, and so was I.

> *All that we see or seem is but a dream within a dream.*
> -Edgar Allan Poe

Chapter XVIV

It is typical of the strange, emotional disease that I have that I can be completely "healthy" – in the moment, feeling my feelings, honest with myself – one minute, and completely sick the next.

My wedding was such a joyous occasion full of so much love and the support of so many friends and family members and I tried to drink it all in through my pores. But after the honeymoon was over and we went back to our jobs and I settled down to the hard work of being a wife and homemaker as well as a full-time employee of a major company, I started to swallow my stress instead of dealing with it. This was complicated by the fact that – although I didn't yet know it – I'd become pregnant shortly after our wedding night. Those unfamiliar hormones were coursing through me, changing me. I began to once again experience dark moods, but felt I couldn't confide them to anyone.

The pregnancy came as wonderful news – the first grandchild on my side of the family – and since the physical changes I was going through accounted for some of my moods, I was able to discount them. I concentrated on eating right and exercising so I would have a healthy baby. My loving husband bought us a waterbed for my birthday, to ease my aching belly and back, and we prepared to welcome a new member of our family.

Meanwhile, every Wednesday night found me at my EA meeting. I was struggling to keep myself together, but it was hard to be serious about my emotions when my swollen stomach was a prime subject of discussion, so I was beginning to let my program lapse. I didn't read from my EA book nightly, as had been my habit, and I didn't call my sponsor quite as often. I was too tired to do much outreach to other members.

The baby, beautiful Andrew, arrived in April, and once again I experienced a joy I'd never known before. What an amazing thing that someone who thought she was destined to spend her life alone should now be holding a perfect newborn, with her husband and family surrounding her. In a way, I thought I'd been suddenly healed from my emotional problems. Maybe I didn't need the program any more. I started skipping meetings – partially because breastfeeding and colic interfered, partially because I didn't want to go.

That was the final straw. A postpartum depression coupled with a very challenging baby who didn't like to sleep much toppled me into the black pit once again. This time my symptoms were subtly different – pervasive anxiety, compulsive thinking and worrying about the baby, crying jags, a feeling that I wasn't really there but floating outside my body. Despite the fact that I'd been through this all before, I ignored my symptoms and suffered silently for a year, confounding my new husband and child. Lucky for me, my depression began to reverse itself just as I slid into my second pregnancy and we prepared to move to a new, larger home.

My emotional "engine light" went on at this point. A marriage, two pregnancies and a move had caused me to hit my stress limit, and I began to start talking to people again, attending meetings, getting back in to the program – finally.

Minds are like parachutes. They only function when they are open.
-James Dewar

Chapter XX

Did you ever notice how real life interferes with happiness? That's how I felt with my lovely little babies – my second, Julie, arrived in August of 1991. I had every reason to be happy, but I was having trouble taking it all in, what with two children sixteen months apart, two sets of diapers to change, a job that I'd switched from full-time to part-time in order to arrange for appropriate caregivers, a new home we'd moved into when Julie was only six weeks old.

I was always short on sleep, and Andrew tested my patience with some strange, attention-getting behaviors and emotional outbursts. I was slowly coming to the realization that I wasn't superwoman – I couldn't handle all this juggling of work, career, mommy responsibilities, wifehood, homemaker. I couldn't be up all night and productive all day and expect to stay sane. I felt like I wanted freeze time for a few days and just enjoy the blessings of my life, but instead I found myself grocery shopping at six in the morning or washing the kitchen floor at midnight, waving to my husband like ships passing in the night.

At this point, we experienced a caregiver crisis that led me to a couple of pivotal decisions in my life. Our primary babysitter needed to retire, and we replaced her with a series of people who didn't work out for one reason or another. I decided that we could no longer leave the care of my son to others – he was going to require a parent at home to aid him in his development – and my daughter was recovering from hospitalization for a severe case of the flu and needed special attention to her diet. I was going to have to quit my job and put my career on hold for a while. The fact that many of my friends and acquaintances seemed to weather similar storms while working full-time made me crazy, but the EA program was helping me try not to compare myself with others but do what is right for me.

We were lucky that my husband's job was secure and lucrative enough to allow us to survive on one paycheck. I resigned, thinking that now all this stress would disappear from my life and I would wake up one morning having changed from a career person to a professional mommy. I was wrong. I plunged into yet another depression, and one evening, covered in vomit and diarrhea from two sick kids and despairing that my hardworking husband was out of town, I lay down on the bathroom floor and cried.

Next morning I put in a call to our doctor for referral to a psychologist. I was going to have to open my mind and heart to another person who could hopefully help me navigate yet another turning point in my life, and this time I had to do it not only for me but for my children and husband.

A promise made is a debt unpaid.
-Robert W. Service

Chapter XXI

It seemed to me that I had been making important promises to people – to my EA friends in commitment to the program, to my husband to be a good wife, to my children to be a good mother. I was even promising not to hold myself to an unachievable standard of perfection – and I wasn't keeping up my end of these bargains. That would have to change.

Although I was fairly good at taking care of my children's physical needs, I sometimes found it difficult to give to them emotionally, probably because I still had my own issues to resolve in counseling. I tried to reverse this pattern by keeping those weekly appointments and supplementing them with my EA meetings. I came to realize that my young son was experiencing physical, developmental and perhaps emotional problems that needed prompt attention, and with the help of this kind counselor, I was able to begin to have these seen to, a process that would take many years. My daughter was doing well, thriving and recovering from her hospitalization, and my husband and I began to make time for each other. We started to go out on dates, cultivated babysitters, took an interest in researching and collecting fine wines, developed our own list of favorite restaurants.

Meanwhile, life was buzzing and humming around us, threatening us with our own mortality. My grandfather was diagnosed with cancer and soon passed away, my father was told his enlarged heart was slowly failing and my mother found she had multiple sclerosis. The complex nature of my sons' condition – he was eventually diagnosed with a mood disorder known as periodic explosive syndrome and helped with therapy and medication – was becoming clearer. I was finding it more and more difficult to get through the day without crying.

I decided to approach my family doctor, who was also a family friend, about medication. I was terrified to take those little pills he told me would help. Day after day I pulled out the bottle of Zoloft (an antidepressant) and simply looked at it and put it back. Finally, one day when my sad moods were more than I could take, I took one. I managed, despite side effects, to take those pills long enough to begin to feel relief. And when it came it flooded me with a sense of well-being that allowed me to redouble my efforts to be the kind of wife, mother and person I knew I could be, and to look at my EA program with a whole new energy. I slept well, started eating right, was less anxious, cried very little, and was able to get out of bed each morning with new hope. When I described my feelings to my husband, Dan, he listened and said, simply, "Carr, that's how I feel most of the time." Finally, I was finding out what normal was. It felt great.

I looked around and discovered that our local EA meeting was dwindling. Some weeks, no one showed up at all. One day a tall, pretty woman who was deep in a series of cyclical depressions that plagued her, came and found Sarah alone at the table. Sarah was able to talk to Lauren quietly, explain the program, help dry her tears, reassure her that there is hope. She also discerned that Lauren and I shared many common interests, including our love of reading, writing and editing publications. She brought us together in what has become one of the most nurturing friendships I've ever experienced. As Lauren worked through dozens of medications – finally finding the one that helped her rise out of that dark pit of despair – we got to know each other and planned fun activities. Or sometimes, when she wasn't feeling up to doing much more than getting out of bed, we simply talked about the EA program and life over the phone. I became her sponsor, which helped me take my twelfth step to a whole new level, and she began tackling steps one, two, three and four with a thoughtful enthusiasm.

As Lauren became more and more well, she, Sarah and I resolved to reinvigorate our little EA meeting. I took over as treasurer and literature person and Lauren made EA flyers to post around the community.

This was to be the start of a wonderful new chapter in our lives that is continuing and evolving to this day, and the conclusion of my first 15 years in the EA program.

You shall have joy, or you shall have power, said God; you shall not have both.
-Ralph Waldo Emerson

Chapter XXII

There are so many kinds of twelve-step programs and so many people needing help (see page 65 for program list). At meetings, we talk to people who are addicted to heroin, booze, cocaine, gambling, food, sex, other people. They are learning to either give up their vices or use them in moderation – learning to say, "I'm powerless over _____." But, they often ask, how can you give up an emotion? How can you use your emotions in moderation? The EA program baffles them, at first, until they realized that it's not about giving up your emotions but giving them over to your higher power.

The AA program says that alcohol is "cunning, baffling and powerful" to those who are addicts; in the same way, emotional illness is overwhelming to those suffering from its effects. The 'cure' for all these addictions is a tough and usually lifelong process. It involves making yourself give to others what you may not have ever received – tenderness, nurturing, compassion, time. Perhaps your parents were alcoholics, maybe they abused you physically or emotionally, maybe you were orphaned and rarely received hugs and kisses, perhaps you've been sickly all your life and never felt the strength of health. Despite all these liabilities, you are called on by the twelve-step programs to perform a miracle – the miracle of helping others achieve what you lacked, and in the process carving out a niche where your self-esteem and serenity can thrive. You build your own house, one brick at a time.

Yes, we are all the product of our genetics and our environment, but that is not all we are. We are spiritual beings who can transcend a botched upbringing or a battered body. By loving others you can learn to love yourself. By trusting others you can learn to trust yourself and your higher power's plan for you. By forgiving others you can forgive yourself, and move on.

I've seen many members come to EA as part of their recovery in other programs. The first step towards kicking drugs might be Narcotics Anonymous, getting yourself clean and sober and able to face the world. The second step might be Emotions Anonymous, dealing with the turbulent feelings that led you to seek solace in oblivion.

It's a long, hard process that seems unfair – why is my life anchored to twelve-step meetings? Why must I perform continuous moral inventories while everyone else I know thrives on lying and cheating and blowing just enough smoke to get by? Why me?

That's the big question. And the answer I've found is surprisingly simple: It doesn't matter why. I can go on whining about why, why, why, or I can get up and do something about it. What matters is what I plan to do with the circumstances in which I find myself, if I can get myself well and reach out to others or if I plan to curl up in a self-pitying ball and wait for my life to end.

I've found I can transcend my past, I can give what I've never received, I can dare to dream big dreams, I can become a better person than I ever thought possible. I can have a life filled with serenity and joy. The catch is, I can't do it on talent and ego and simple perseverance. Those things haven't worked for me and I can't control the power I let them have in my life.

I have to remember that I must lean on God and EA to stand up straight. That knowledge is my power.

> With the ancient is wisdom; and in length of days understanding.
> -Bible, Book of Proverbs, Job 12

Chapter XXIII

Oh, those comforting traditions of childhood. I remember the trips to Grandma's on Christmas Eve; holiday breakfasts at the neighbor's, special ceremonies marking religious occasions. Sameness made me feel safe, and from that safety I could learn to grow and take chances.

Religious ceremonies have that sense of familiarity, too, proceeding with their rituals in predictable patterns. From the Jewish celebration of Hanukkah to the African-American's Kwanzaa, and even to an atheist's joy in marking the winter and summer solstices, we are a people of tradition.

The EA program, I've found, also relies on the consistency of ceremony. There is an approved written format for meetings, and members greet each other in a traditional way. Most meetings - other than special public information or speaker meetings - proceed along the same lines each week, starting with members reading from a yellow pamphlet that includes guidelines for the program (see epilogue).

When I first started coming to EA, I found these traditions odd and their repetition somewhat boring. Now I barely notice the meeting format, and when I do, it is with that same feeling of comfort that came from my childhood traditions. I feel safe here, safe in the sameness, and able to take risks and grow. Also, the repetitive nature of the readings allows a sense of serenity to take hold in me, and I often "hear" a certain phrase or step in a new way, even though I'd read it a hundred times before.

Newcomers to EA sometimes expect to see seriously troubled people, barely able to cope. They are surprised to recognize others like themselves, all races, sexes, backgrounds and sexual preferences. And while no one comes to EA because they are particularly happy with their lives, everyone's emotional histories are unique. Yes, we've welcomed very disturbed individuals just out of mental hospitals, but mostly, we see your average young mother, retiree, middle-aged businessman. Everyone is encouraged to share their thoughts or feelings about the step we're discussing for the evening, but no one is advised to wallow in their own regrets, sorrow and sadness.

We can't give advice on how you should solve your problems, but we encourage a focus on the positive – the solution – rather than the negative. Everything said at a meeting is confidential and your complete anonymity is assured. You are accepted for who you are and encouraged to become who you believe you can be.

EA may not be the magic bullet for everyone, but I can't imagine my life without it. Keep coming back, we say. It works if you work it. And you add a lot of love.

Epilogue

Selected tenets of EA's twelve-step program reprinted courtesy of EA International Services Center, P.O. Box 4245, St. Paul, MN 55104-0245, USA, phone (651) 647-9712, fax (651) 647-1593. Copyright, 1972 Emotions Anonymous. Revised 1994. Contact the Emotions Anonymous web page at http://www.mtn.org/EA, or send an email message to eaisc@mtn.org

The Twelve Steps of EA

1. We admitted we were powerless over our emotions – that our lives had become unmanageable.
2. Came to believe that a Power greater than ourselves could restore us to sanity.
3. Made a decision to turn our will and our lives over to the care of God as we understood Him.
4. Made a searching and fearless moral inventory of ourselves.
5. Admitted to God, to ourselves and to another human being the exact nature of our wrongs.
6. Were entirely ready to have God remove all these defects of character.
7. Humbly asked Him to remove our shortcomings.
8. Made a list of all persons we had harmed and became willing to make amends to them all.

9. Made direct amend to such people wherever possible, except when to do so would injure them or others.
10. Continued to take personal inventory and when we were wrong promptly admitted it.
11. Sought through prayers and meditation to improve our conscious contact with God as we understood Him, praying only for knowledge of His will for us and the power to carry that out.
12. Having had a spiritual awakening as a result of these steps, we tried to carry this message and practice these principles in all our affairs.

The Twelve Promises of EA

1. We realize a new freedom and happiness.
2. We do not regret the past or wish to shut the door on it.
3. We comprehend the word serenity, and we know peace of mind.
4. No matter how far down the scale we have gone, we see how our experience can benefit others.
5. The feelings of uselessness and self-pity lessen.
6. We have less concern about self and gain interest in others.
7. Self-seeking slips away.
8. Our whole attitude and outlook upon life changes.
9. Our relationships with other people improve.
10. We intuitively know how to handle situations which used to baffle us.
11. We acquire a feeling of security within ourselves.
12. We realize that God is doing for us what we could not do ourselves.

Slogans We Use

1. Let go and let God.
2. You are not alone.

3. One day at a time.
4. Live and let live.
5. First things first.
6. Look for the good.
7. By the grace of God.
8. Know yourself – be honest.
9. This too shall pass.
10. I need people.
11. Keep it simple.
12. I have a choice.

Just For Today
(The Choice Is Mine)

1. Just for today I will try to live through this day only, not tackling all of my problems at once. I can do something at this moment that would discourage me if I had to continue it for a lifetime.
2. Just for today I will try to be happy, realizing my happiness does not depend on what others do or say or what happens around me. Happiness is a result of being at peace with myself.
3. Just for today I will try to adjust myself to what is and not force everything to adjust to my own desires. I will accept my family, my friends, my business, my circumstances as they come.
4. Just for today I will take care of my physical health; I will exercise my mind: I will read something spiritual.
5. Just for today I will do somebody a good turn and not get found out. If anyone knows of it, it will not count. I will do at least one thing I don't want to do, and I will perform some small act of love for my neighbor.
6. Just for today I will try to go out of my way to be kind to someone I meet. I will be considerate, talk low, and look as good as I can. I will not engage in unnecessary

criticism or finding fault, nor try to improve or regulate anybody except myself.
7. Just for today I will have a program. I may not follow it exactly, but I will have it. I will save myself from two pests – hurry and indecision.
8. Just for today I will stop saying, "If I had time." I never will find time for anything. If I want time, I must take it.
9. Just for today I will have a quiet time of meditation wherein I shall think of my Higher power, of myself, and of my neighbor. I shall relax and seek truth.
10. Just for today I shall be unafraid. Particularly, I shall be unafraid to be happy, to enjoy what is good, what is beautiful, and what is lovely in life.
11. Just for today I will not compare myself with others. I will accept myself and live to the best of my ability.
12. Just for today I choose to believe that I can live this one day.

Welcome to a New Way of Life
(Pamphlet for newcomers)

Emotions Anonymous is a fellowship of people of all ages and backgrounds who come together to share personal experiences and hope as we work toward recovery from various emotional difficulties. We learn how to live a new way of life by using the twelve steps of the program to help us find serenity and peace of mind.

Everyone is welcome to attend EA meetings. The only requirement for membership is the desire to become well emotionally. EA might have just what you need at this point in your life.

You may be surprised to meet many happy, healthy, well-adjusted people here, yet no one first attended a meeting because he or she was happy. Some people came to EA because life was simply uncomfortable and they were looking for a better way. Others have been in the depths of despair, been in therapy or perhaps hospitalized.

What all members have in common is that this program works to change their lives. Our program has worked miracles in the lives of many who suffer from such emotional problems as excessive anger and resentment, depression, low self-esteem, guilt, grief, anxiety, obsessive and negative thinking, panic, phobias and compulsive behaviors.

As an anonymous organization, the confidentiality of our members is respected at all times. It is entirely up to us what we choose to tell other members about ourselves. This anonymity also gives us the freedom to share our thoughts and feelings at meetings because what is said there is not to be repeated to anyone else.

All participation at EA meetings is voluntary. No one is required to talk or to give personal information. However, if we wish to, we share about our own personal experiences and feelings and how we use the program. EA provides a warm and accepting group setting in which to share without fear of criticism. Through weekly meetings we discover we are not alone in our struggles, and we find caring individuals to support our recovery.

At our meetings we do not discuss religion, politics, national or international issues or other belief systems because EA has no opinion on outside issues. We avoid discussing the problems of others or complaining about people in our lives. We discuss only the EA program. It is up to individual members to determine what course of action may or may not be appropriate for themselves regarding any religious belief, therapy, medication or mental health issue.

Emotions Anonymous is not a medical or psychiatric service, nor does it provide personal or family counseling. Our meetings are conducted by EA members, not professionals. Medical, social service or religious professionals do not lead meetings but may attend and participate as fellow EA members. Leadership at group meetings rotates. The function of the leader is only to conduct the meeting, not to serve as any kind of authority or expert.

As a spiritual program, there is emphasis on a personal higher power, a power greater than ourselves, to whom we may turn for direction in our lives. Everyone has the personal choice of what this power may be. The EA program works for those holding various formal religious beliefs or for those with no religious beliefs.

Emotions Anonymous is a non-profit organization supported by the voluntary contributions of its members. No financial support is accepted from outside sources. Donations are collected at each meeting to cover the expenses for maintaining our organization.

This program has helped thousands of people since it was founded in 1971. Today Emotions Anonymous can be found throughout the United States and in many other countries. We hope you will give this program a chance to be helpful for you by attending our meetings. We suggest you attend several meetings before deciding if Emotions Anonymous can give the support and help you may be seeking.

National Service Centers For Various Twelve-Step Programs Nationwide

Below are fellowships similar to the AA/EA model that you may find to be helpful in your recovery. This information is courtesy the New Jersey Self-Help Clearinghouse and is subject to change.

Adult Children of Alcoholics
World Service Organization
P.O. Box 3216
Torrance, CA 90510
Phone 310-534-1815

Al-Anon/Alateen Family Groups
1600 Corporate Landing Parkway
Virginia Beach, VA 23454-5617
Phone 1-800-356-9996

Alcoholics Anonymous
General Service Office
Phone 212-870-3400

A.R.T.S. Anonymous (Artists recovering through the twelve steps)
P.O. Box 175 – Ansonia Station
New York, NY 10023
Phone 212-873-7075

Clutterers Anonymous
P.O. Box 25884
Santa Ana, CA 92799-5884
No Phone Number

Cocaine Anonymous
9100 Sepulveda Blvd. Suite 216
Los Angeles, CA 90045
Phone 310-216-4444

Co-Dependents Anonymous (CODA)
P.O. Box 33577
Phoenix, AZ 85067-3577
Phone 602-277-7991

Debtors Anonymous
P.O. Box 400
New York, NY 10163-0040
No phone number

Gamblers Anonymous
P.O. Box 17173
Los Angeles, CA 90017
Phone 213-386-8789

Incest Survivors Anonymous
P.O. Box 17245
Long Beach, CA 90807-7245
No phone number

Narcotics Anonymous
World Service Office, Inc.
P.O. Box 9999
Van Nuys, CA 91409-9999
Phone 818-787-7189

Nicotine Anonymous
P.O. Box 591777
San Francisco, CA 94159-1777
Phone 415-750-0328

Obsessive-Compulsives Anonymous
P.O. Box 215
New Hyde Park, NY 11040
Phone 516-741-4901

Overeaters Anonymous
P.O. Box 44020
Rio Rancho, NM 87174
Phone 505-292-9080

Sex Addicts Anonymous
P.O. Box 70949
Houston, TX 77270
Phone 713-869-4902

Contact the American Self-Help Clearinghouse at (73) 652-9565 for additional self-help programs.

If you'd like to order additional copies of this book, fill out the order form on page 70. Also, I would like to pursue a follow-up to this book that focuses on your stories about EA and other twelve-step programs. Send your stories to P.O. Box 31613, Independence, Ohio, 44131-0613. Include a self-addressed, stamped envelope to find out whether your story is selected for inclusion.

About the author

Carrie Connelly, a pseudonym used by the author to protect anonymity according to EA tradition, is a freelance writer with 20 years of experience writing and editing newspapers, newsletters and magazines. She is 40 years old and lives with her husband and two children in Ohio. She is a long-time member of the twelve-step program Emotions Anonymous. This is her first book. Half of the profits from the sale of this book will be donated to Emotions Anonymous International.

Order Form

To order additional copies, fill out this form and send it along with your check or money order to: P.O. Box 31613, Independence, Ohio, 44131-0613.

Cost per copy $5.50 plus $2.00 postage. If shipped to an address in Ohio, include 7% State sales tax.

Ship _____ copies of *Like A Shoe That Pinches* to:

Name_____

_____

_____

Phone:_____